TOP SECRETS
REVEALED

21 WAYS TO STOP GUMBORO DISEASE
FAILURE IN YOUR POULTRY FARM

YILKES ZUMUNCI BITRUS

21 WAYS TO STOP CUMBORO DISEASE FAILURE IN YOUR POULTRY FARM

By

Yilkes Zumunci Bitrus

ISBN: 9798858065296

All Enquiries To
+234 903 647 3111
Email: Yilkeszumunci2@gmail. com

Designed, @DgalaGraphiz
Email: dgala0019@gmail.com
+234 (0)8147163578 +234 (0)7052404294

DEDICATION

I dedicate this book to God almighty who has given me the knowledge and wisdom in life. I also appreciate the patient of my wife and children who believe my knowledge should be shared to people all over the world.

TABLE OF CONTENTS

INTRODUCTION

Poultry industry is among the profitable and lucrative ventures all over the world, however, it's been deterred by certain diseases. One among the 'chiefest' is 'Gumboro disease (infectious bursal disease IBD).

It is a viral disease which spread fast by contact among the birds as well as ingesting the infected faecal stool. Vaccines are there to offer protection against the disease; howbeit some factors could make it "fail" or not giving the protection as the case may be. This could make a poultry farmer attract a colossal lost in the farm due to losses and damage which in turn could bring dissatisfaction and depression to the farmer.

In Gumboro disease scenario, Morbidity is high which mortality could range from low to high. Morbidity means the rate of the birds having the infection while mortality means death rate.

In this book, I'm going to show you what is Gumboro disease, how you can avoid it in your poultry farm and the remedy, should it occur in your farm.

GUMBORO VACCINE

This is a live vaccine that comprises a virulent virus whose pathogenicity has been weakened through consecutive cultures in living cells but the virus maintains its immunogenic antigenicity for stimulating the body's immune response: this whole process is commonly known as attenuation.

WHAT IS GUMBORO VACCINE FAILURE

Vaccine failure is the consequence of the inability of the chicken to develop adequate immunity after immunization or susceptibility of bird to field outbreak after administration of the vaccine. High rate of 56.7% of vaccination failure has been recorded in vaccinated poultry flocks in Nigeria. The common breaches in transportation, handing, storage and administration are the high rates, responsible for the Gumboro vaccine failure in poultry industry.

BURSA OF FABRICIUS

This is a structure or an organ in the body of a bird that is responsible for regulating or controlling the effect of Gumboro disease.

Bursa of fabricius is a chestnut – size, sac like organ located dorsal (backward) to the rectum of a chicken. It is a lymphoid organ that is responsible for development of adaptive immunity. It controls antibody-mediated immunity in young birds. The bursa regresses with age and thus its presence or absence may be used to determine the age of the bird. The older the bird, the more its bursa of fabricius disappears, vice versa.

HISTORY OF GUMBORO

Gumboro was first discovered in USA. In 1950s, people of certain town called "Gumboro" were known for a peculiar disease that kill their birds, that people in the neighboring towns, cities and villages of America started making fun of them, in the course of time and events, people of "Gumboro "town started "migrating ", to other places in the America with their fowls (birds) as gifts or to sell.

People started noticing some strange and incurable disease peculiar to the birds that were migrated from "Gumboro" town. This triggered Dr. Albert S. Cosgrove and Hiram N. Lasher at Delaware (Millsboro) in 1957 to set up laboratory asylum to work on why birds from Gumboro town are having peculiar infection. The research process took tem 5 to 6 years to ascertain the cause. In 1962, they discovered that a virus is responsible for the high death of fowl (birds) of the "Gumboro "town people thus, common to young (chicks), which attack their bursa of fabricius (located inside the vent area of a bird). They called it infectious bursal disease (IBD) which people nicked named ("Gumboro Disease ") since it came from Gumboro town. The disease is now found all over the world except in New Zealand.

THE CAUSE OF GUMBORO "(IBD)

It is caused by a virus called Avibinavirus.

NB: No cure to any viral disease, you only manage and treat secondary bacterial infections.

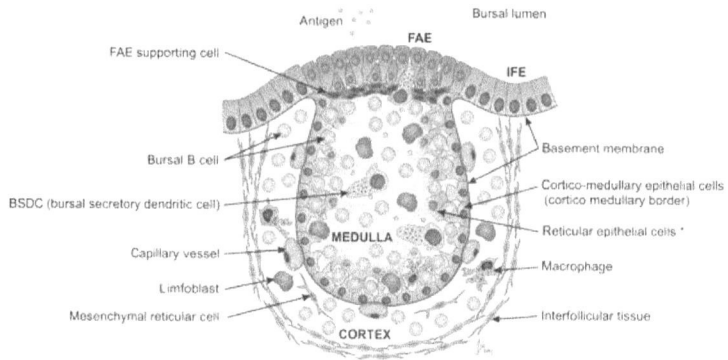

THE DIAGRAM OF BURSA OF FIBRICIUS

MODE OF TRANSMISSION

The disease is transferred easily to other birds through:

I.   Stool (faeces)

II.   Feed

III.   Water

IV.   Bedding materials litter / wood – shavings in the house.

V. Apparatus / equipment use/ within the poultry house

VI. People / Animals in and around poultry farms

VII. Vehicles/ physical contact.

CAN IT AFFECT HUMAN?

The answer is no. it has never been transmitted to human. Or other animals. It is not a zoonotic disease.

SOME NAMES RELATED TO GUMBORO DISEASES

a) infectious bursal disease (IBD)

b) infectious bursitis

c) infectious avian neurosis

d) " farm wiper disease " (because it can clear the whole flock)

HOW CAN I PREVENT GUMBORO DISEASE IN MY FARM?

Only through vaccination and biosecurity.

CAN BIRDS (CHICKS) COME WITH GUMBORO DISEASE FROM THE HATCHERY?

The answer to this is NO. There is no vertical transmission

COMMON SIGNS TO KNOW YOUR BIRDS ARE WITH GUMBORO DISEASE.

a) Ruffled feathers

b) Wearing coat "and drowsy.

c) Not feeding properly./anoraxea

d) " sleepy " and huddling in clusters (group) even when you put source of heat to them

e) Wet vent

f) Mixed stool (whitish, brownish, e.t.c)

g) Depression or listless.

h) Sleeping with their beaks touching the ground.

i) Tremor.

POST – MORTEM EXMINATION (PM)

Three (3) basic alerts or notifications you will see obviously that are related to the post – mortem (pm) lesions:

1. Inflamed bursa of Fabricius

2. Muscular haemorhages (stains of blood in the muscles)

3. Linear hemorrhages around the proventriculus.

4. Emaciated and dehydrated carcass due to lack of feed and water intake.

5. Inflamed urates.

REASONS WHY GUMBORO FAIL

Gumboro - failure means the Gumboro (IBDV) vaccines administered has failed to protect the birds against Gumboro disease. This could be as a result of some factors as follows:

1. **Genetic factors**: bird might be more susceptible to pathogen due to the lack of some structure in MHC (Major his to compatibility complex). The birds are predisposing to higher immune depletion, thereby, causing more death on the birds. Some birds are more susceptible to Gumboro disease than others due to genetic factors or conditions. Naturally some birds are having weaker immune system thus, making the T Cells of the bursa of Fabricius less active to combat or resist the disease strain.

2. **Lack of maintaining cold – chain of vaccines**: No Gumboro - Vaccine should be given to birds without been preserved in a suitable temperature recommended by the manufacturer. (To be stored in refrigerators). The rule says the desired temperature should be kept and maintained from the manufacturer to the farmer. Once the cold chain of the vaccine is broken, the vaccine gets denatured, thus, become useless to the system of the bird.

NB: Gumboro vaccines are live vaccines, if failed to be preserved in a right sequence / temperature, the bird automatically come down with the Gumboro disease after administering (4 - 7 days).

3. **Coccidiosis in birds:** Ensure there is no sign of coccidiosis disease in your birds

before you administer Gumboro vaccines. Treat all traces of coccidiosis before administering the vaccine. Coccidiosis is a blood – related protozoan infection that would neutralize your vaccine, since blood remains the carrier or means of transportation of vaccines to their respective sites. This is the common of all causes – take note please.

4. **Lack of adhering to the manufacturer's instructions**: Your Gumboro vaccines could fail when you failed to adhere /abide by the owner's simple instructions. Instructions like: route of vaccines administration (intramscular, subcutaneous, intravenous) oral route (p/0) using wrong diluent to reconstitute your vaccines etc.

5. **Expired vaccines:** Always ensure your vaccines are valid in dates. Always get your vaccines from a certified vet. and trust worthy Centers. Always check expiring date.

6. **Putting Gumboro vaccines in offensive containers**: This is common when you are buying from vendor that mix and sell to customers. Avoid using containers that were used for other products to collect your vaccines. Example: alcoholic containers, chemical containers, smelled containers etc. You must wash your container to be used for collection of vaccines overnight allows it to dry before the following day. Offensive containers usually neutralize the potency of your vaccine.

7. **Inadequate dosage:** When giving oral vaccines especially, ensure you add more containers (x2 of water you already have, their drinkers). Insufficient drinkers could lead to not all the birds taking the vaccines, thereby causing more harm to the system.

8. **Before giving oral Gumboro Vaccines, ensure you starve the birds of water over night.** Always ensure you deny your birds water over the night if you are administratering oral vaccines. This will make the birds thirsty not to delay in taking the vaccines.

9. **Avoid delay**: Every reconstituted (mixed) vaccine should and must be given to the birds in less than an hour.

10. **Avoid shaking of Gumboro vaccine:** Every live vaccine should not be "shaken ", avoid carrying your vaccines in "Jerrycans ". That is the mixed vaccines, or avoid conveying the mixed Gumboro vaccine to a long distance.

NB: It's better not to administer Gumboro vaccine to your birds if you live in a far distant area from point of vaccine collection centre to your farm, than giving a denatured vaccine – it could be disastrous and the death of your chicken could be colossal.

11. **Reduce the hot temperature in your poultry pen**: This is common during raining season when farmers could still be "heating "their poultry pen up to a week or so. This hot temperature in the body of the chicken could neutralize your Gumboro

vaccines. Avoid by all means, not to increase the body temperature of your birds during vaccination.

12. **Government policy**: Failure of government to enact – laws on vaccine carriage, no regulatory vaccine body to check – mate who and who are qualify to sell or give vaccines.

13. **Don't administrate Gumboro vaccine to your birds if you pick any mortality from the flock 2 or 3 days prior to the date of giving vaccines**. Suspend given vaccines when you pick a dead chicken within the week of vaccine
administration. Please go for poste- mortem (PM) immediately.

14. **Avoid mixing of different vaccine companies together:** Not all company's antigens can tolerated or accommodate

other company's antigens. Avoid mixing two or more different Gumboro vaccine companies together.

15. **Age aggregate**: The age bracket of your birds matter alot in giving Gumboro vaccines within 1 – 4 weeks of age. Avoid giving Gumboro vaccines from 5 weeks upward, because the cover that the vaccine is to give, must have formed resistant in the bursa of fabricius.

16. **Not getting the right dose and dosage:** Giving under dose or overdoes can cause Gumboro failure.

17. **Please avoid giving any form of antibiotics or anti coccidiousis treatment in the week that you administered Gumboro vaccines to the same birds:** Any treatment should be after a week;

hence, you break or annul your given Gumboro vaccine.

18. **Avoid mixing Gumboro vaccine together with any type vaccine to be administered at the same time or same day. Avoid it completely.**

19. **Avoid excess load of litter in the poultry pen:** Excess manure can harbor diseases or parasites that can in turn, cause vaccines failure.

20. **Maternal anti bodies / immunity**: Hatched chicks are passively immunized due to maternal antibodies in their blood. The maternal antibodies have potential to interact with the vaccine antigens and result in neutralizing antigen. Thus, vaccines such as live vaccines (Gumboro) affect the developmental of immunity production by reducing the level of anti

bodies in the newly hatched chicks if they are vaccinated for first weeks.

21. **Difference in serotype:** Serotypes differs from area-to-area identification of locally circulating infectious agent in different areas are most important for vaccine production. Thus, these locally isolated antigens (immunogens) are used for manufacturing of vaccines.

Disease outbreak can occur in the area if these locally antigens are not used during the Gumboro vaccines production. Most imported vaccines may contain serotypes that differ from the circulating local or field strain and may not be effective to tackle high virulent strains of different nature.

Good to know that you are still following, understanding as well as enjoying this book. Listen! 90% of Gumboro failures occur after the second dose of the Gumboro administration. Please pay serious attention to hear, learn and act from this.

Most poultry owners would tell the truth from this aspect: 'Second Shot' or Dosage of the Gumboro vaccines are the most common and easier one that fail – usually given from 2nd or 3rd weeks of age of the birds. Do you know why it fails so easily from the mentioned period? I will tell you pls.

The reason is simple. From second or third weeks, coccidiosis tend to set in the farm and immediately Gumboro vaccine is administered on coccidiosis birds, it neutralize all your Gumboro vaccine and within days or week after administration of the vaccine. The birds would start clustering in groups, as if cold is catching them, they become inactive, less buy, less appetite and sleepy with their feather ruffled or as if they are wearing coat.

Coccidiosis is the major reason why Gumboro vaccines usually fail in the farm - please take note and handle this with all seriousness and be more conscious of this.

Coccidiosis is a blood – related infection in poultry farm, it acts on the blood of the animal. This is why coccidiosis poses a great threat and challenge to Gumboro vaccines failure:

Blood to every living creature serves as a medium of transportation. Since everything that enters the system of an animal, blood tend, to be its medium of transportation, imagine now that the blood is infected with coccidiosis, this means that the medium or channel of our transportation is faulty. Coccidiosis causing agents (Eimeria app), which is found and act on the blood vessels, or release exude their infectious substances on our Gumboro vaccines thereby , destroying the active ingredient that is found in the Gumboro vaccine, thereby, annulling or neutralizing the vaccines efficiency hence, the Gumboro vaccines become impotent or got denatured. Which simple means, the vaccine become useless at the moment and it's no longer useful again in the body of the birds.

Please note that when viral base vaccines like Gumboro vaccines, Newcastle disease vaccine (Lasota), Marek's vaccines, Fowl pox vaccines e.t.c. Once they are denatured or render impotent, if given animals in (poultry) or disease automatically: because virus don't die.

Please read this module over and over again until you capture every nounce in it – very important please!!!

This is one of the secrets where most farmers lay blames on either the source of the vaccines or they accuse their Vet. Personnel of bringing a fake vaccine to them, not knowing the fault is none either way. Let me show you simple ways you can know whether the vaccines failure comes from within the farm or from outside (as in lack of cold chain, mishandling, see some factors highlighted above.

SOME IMPORTANT THINGS TO NOTE ON VACCINES.

1. Vaccines are not drugs or chemical. Don't' use vaccines to treat your livestocks.

2. The best time to give / administer vaccine in your farm is early morning or late evening - avoid hot temperature when giving vaccines.

3. Avoid pouring left – over vaccines around your farm. Live vaccines can be spread easily and faster within farms – rather, dig a hole to bury left – over vaccines in the farms, especially, Gumboro vaccines.

4. Handle all vaccines with care and always abide by the Manufacturer's instructions – caveat emptor".

5. Buy vaccines only from certified / qualified vendors. Avoid quacks.

6. Avoids borrowing vaccines from neighboring farms.

7. **Please note that once a farm is having Gumboro disease history, it can occur again time to time in the farm**.

8. Don't administer Gumboro vaccines again to the birds that have Gumboro failure subsequently. Take note please.

WHAT TO DO IF YOU HAVE GUMBORO DISEASE IN YOUR POULTRY FARM.

You found out that despite all protective measures, one may still come down with the disease in his / her farm due to factors like: Serendipity, measures beyond human control, insufficient information and technology, over confidence from the farmer, "fake and denature vaccines, wrong dosage or under diluting the vaccines, not having enough or insufficient drinkers to distribute the mixed vaccines.

CERTAIN MEASURES OF CONTROL AND MANAGEMENT ARE TO BE DONE:

❖ Cull and isolate the infected birds. Ensure that the birds you noticed with the Gumboro disease signs are removed and isolated in a separate room or environment so as to reduce the spread easily – Quarantine.

❖ Ensure a good bio – security measure. Restrict people from in and out of your farm. Ensure their drinkers and feeders are cleaned and disinfected.

❖ Treat Gumboro case using the " Halogens." These are group of element in the periodic table that their ways of action are needed by the birds in minute quantity – thus, very effective. Example include: iodine, chlorine etc.

There are other group of substances that paliate or subside the virulence of Gumboro disease e.g. King – Herbs, Gumbo – ND, Super viral etc.

❖ Ensure good open – crossed – ventilation. At this time their immune system is compromised therefore, different signs would be noticed in the pen. Good crossed – ventilation will release them of further stress.

❖ Spray. There are different spraying – agent that will arrest further spread within the farm among the birds, example you can use (sawke) iodine – liquid and spray while the birds are inside – meaning, you get a sprayer and dilute about 20ml of sawke to 10 or liters of water, mix it in the sprayer and spray the whole pen with the birds inside the pen.

Note please – if Gomboro failure occurs in your farm between 2wks – 6wks of age, you must / should definitely check the menace of coccidiosis and include it in your line of treatment. It is the common trigger factors among the cause of high mortality on the on- set.

Coccidiosis in young chicks is the triggering factors why morality go up in geometrical ratio. Take note. Until you handle coccidiosis, the mortality would keep increasing. I feel like to add this……

❖ Use a positive affirmation in your farm always. You are your words. Words are powerful. Life and death are in the mouth. Don't say or profess negative statement on your birds. Confession brings possession .you see what you say with your mouth always. Always pray to God for protection and guidance over your birds for God's safety.

CONCLUSION

Don't give up in life. Afflictions are bound to come our ways sometimes, as test and trials – don't give up. You may have lost huge capital invested in a poultry venture, please don't give up, better days are soon coming.

Gomboro disease (infectious Bursal Disease IBD) has caused colossal lost and damage, if not bankruptcy to many individuals as a result of lack of adequate knowledge or information, sufficiently about the disease. Adhering to the simple but thorough concepts written in this E-book, you stand the chance of eradicating this lethal disease in your farm – Gomboro disease.

Gomboro disease is like a car that got an accident that keeps summersaulting, all efforts to stop it at once might not be feasible, but with one or two "wedge", it will definitely come to halt.

www.ingramcontent.com/pod-product-compliance
Lightning Source LLC
Chambersburg PA
CBHW072225290526
45794CB00007B/2894